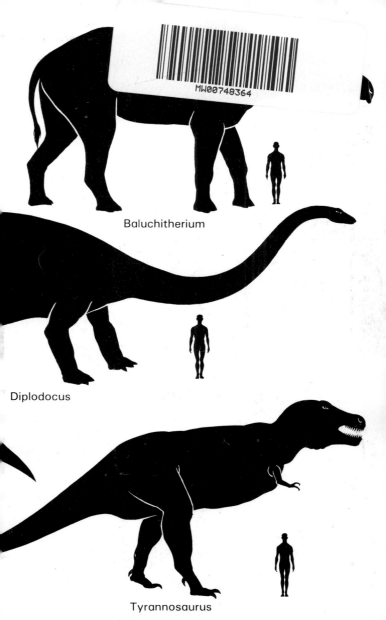

Baluchitherium

Diplodocus

Tyrannosaurus

Ladybird books are widely available, but in case of
difficulty may be ordered by post or telephone from:

Ladybird Books – Cash Sales Department
Littlegate Road  Paignton  Devon TQ3 3BE
Telephone 0803 554761

A catalogue record for this book is available
from the British Library

Published by Ladybird Books Ltd  Loughborough  Leicestershire  UK
Ladybird Books Inc  Auburn  Maine 04210  USA

# DINOSAURS

Adapted by Ben M Baglio
from Colin Douglas's original text

Illustrated by B H Robinson

Ladybird

Once the Earth was very hot. As it slowly cooled, rain began to fall. The rain water made rivers and

oceans. Nothing lived on the land
or in the sea. There were no
plants, no animals and no people.

# Life began in the sea

Trilobite
(try-lo-bite)

Sponges

The first plants were *algae* and the first animals were tiny creatures called *protozoa*. Over millions of years, the animals changed into

Belemnite

Jellyfish

Ammonite

Starfish

jellyfish and sponges. Later,
there were worms and starfish.
Later still, there were animals
that had shells.

# The age of fish

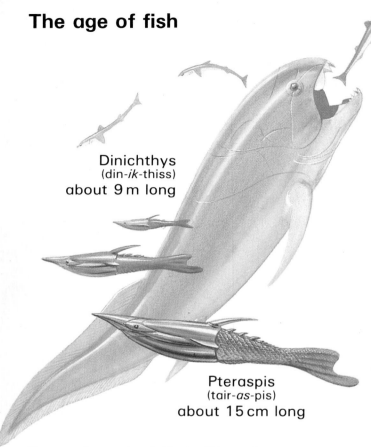

Dinichthys
(din-*ik*-thiss)
about 9 m long

Pteraspis
(tair-*as*-pis)
about 15 cm long

Bony-headed fish like these
began to live in the sea. Most,
like Pteraspis, were quite small,
but Dinichthys was as long as a
bus!

At this time, plants began to grow on the land. They looked like the mosses and ferns we see today, but some were as tall as trees.

# Onto the land

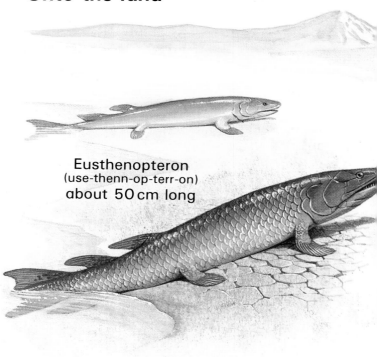

Eusthenopteron
(use-thenn-op-terr-on)
about 50 cm long

Slowly, the Earth's climate
became hotter again, and many
lakes and rivers dried up. Some
fish, like Eusthenopteron, grew
lungs and very strong fins so that
they could crawl onto the land.

# The first amphibians (am-fib-y-ans)

Ichthyostega
(ik-thee-o-*stee*-ga)
about 1 m long

Millions of years later, some fish grew legs. They had become amphibians. This means that they could live both on land and in water.

Eryops
(*air*-ee-ops)
about 2 m long

As time went by, many different
kinds of amphibians appeared.
Some were only 5 cm long.
Others, like Eogyrinus, grew as
long as 4.5 m.

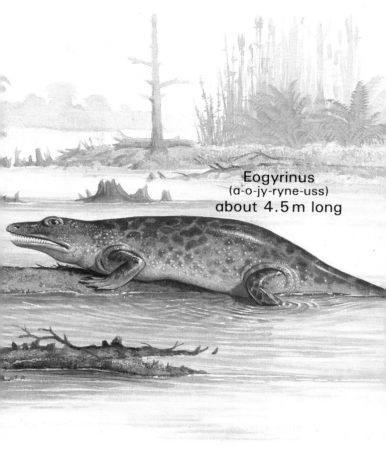

Eogyrinus
(a-o-jy-ryne-uss)
about 4.5 m long

Amphibians ruled the Earth for many millions of years. But as the climate became drier, slowly, some amphibians changed into reptiles.

# The first reptiles

Seymouria
(see-*more*-ee-ya)
about 60 cm long

Unlike amphibians, reptiles do
not need to go into water to lay
eggs. The females lay waterproof
eggs on land. Seymouria was
one of the first reptiles.

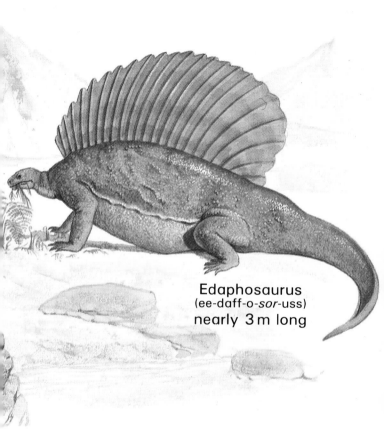

Edaphosaurus
(ee-daff-o-*sor*-uss)
nearly 3 m long

Reptiles began to look less like
amphibians. Some, like
Edaphosaurus, grew large fins on
their backs. These fins could be
up to 2 m high.

# Dimetrodon

(di-*mee*-trow-don)
about 3 m long

Dimetrodon was one of the first
reptiles to eat meat. It ate
smaller amphibians and reptiles.

# An amphibian and a reptile of today

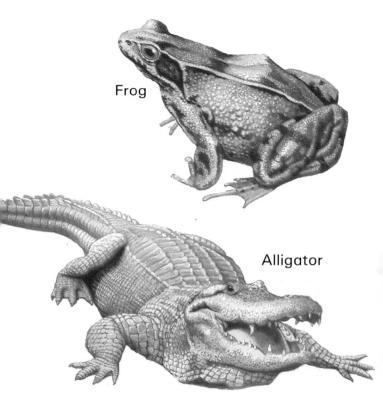

Frog

Alligator

There are still reptiles and
amphibians on Earth today. The
frog is an amphibian. It lays its
eggs in water. The alligator is a
reptile. It lays its eggs on land.

# Sea reptiles

Ichthyosaurus
(ik-thee-o-*sor*-uss)
between 3 and 12 m long

Some reptiles went back to live
in the water. They did not lay
eggs. The young sea reptiles
hatched from eggs *inside* the
mother's body.

Plesiosaurus
(pless-i-o-*sor*-uss)
about 12 m long

Ichthyosaurus looked like a dolphin
and could swim very fast to catch
fish to eat. Plesiosaurus could not
swim fast. Its very long neck
helped it to find food.

19

# Gliding reptiles

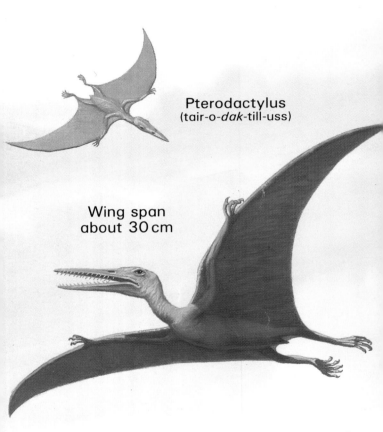

Pterodactylus
(tair-o-*dak*-till-uss)

Wing span
about 30 cm

Some reptiles grew wings which
were made of a thin layer of
skin. These let them glide
through the air. Some of these

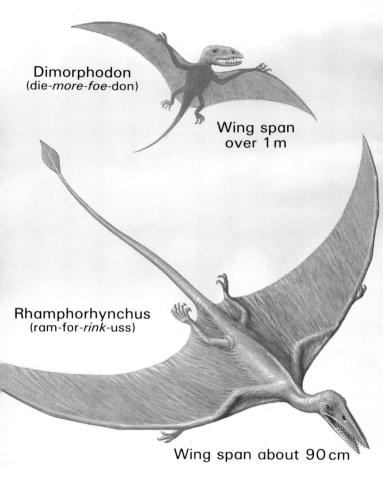

Dimorphodon
(die-*more-foe*-don)

Wing span
over 1 m

Rhamphorhynchus
(ram-for-*rink*-uss)

Wing span about 90 cm

reptiles were enormous, but
many were no larger than a
small bird. Gliding reptiles ate
fish or small reptiles and insects.

# Pteranodon
(tair-ran-o-don)

Pteranodon was one of the
biggest gliding reptiles. Its wing
span could be as wide as 8 m.
Gliding reptiles lived on cliffs
near the sea.

Wing span up to 8 m

23

# Footprints from the past

Very large bones were found in England during the 1820s. Later, huge footprints were found both in England and in America.

Skeleton of Apatosaurus

The footprints and bones were those of a dinosaur. They had been buried in the ground and *preserved* for millions of years.

The word dinosaur means "terrible lizard".

# Diplodocus and Apatosaurus

There were many kinds of dinosaurs, and they all lived long before the first humans. Some were very small and quick, but others were very big and slow.

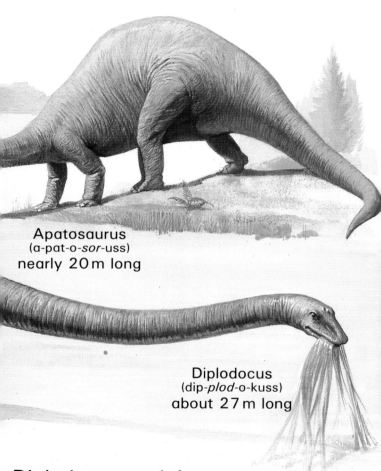

Apatosaurus
(a-pat-o-*sor*-uss)
nearly 20 m long

Diplodocus
(dip-*plod*-o-kuss)
about 27 m long

Diplodocus and Apatosaurus
were two of the biggest
dinosaurs. They were gentle
plant-eaters and lived in herds for
protection.

27

# Stegosaurus and Allosaurus

Stegosaurus
(steg-o-*sor*-uss)
about 6 m long

Stegosaurus was very slow. It had bony plates and a spiked tail to protect it from its enemies.

Allosaurus
(al-lo-*sor*-uss)
over 9 m long

Allosaurus was a large meat-
eating dinosaur that stood on
two legs. Its mouth opened so
wide that it could swallow small
animals whole.

# Hypsilophodon and Iguanodon

Hypsilophodon
(hip-sill-loff-o-don)
up to 2 m long

Hypsilophodon was a very small dinosaur but it could move quickly on two legs to escape from its enemies.

Iguanodon
(ig-*wan*-o-don)
over 9 m long

Iguanodon was a much larger
plant-eater. It had a bony spike
on each thumb that it used to
fight off its attackers.

# Polacanthus

(poll-a-kan-thuss)
about 4 m long

Remains of Polacanthus were found in England. The double row of spikes on its back and the bony plates on its tail kept other animals away.

# Ankylosaurus

(an-*kile*-lo-*sor*-uss)
over 4.5 m long

Ankylosaurus appeared on Earth
later than Stegosaurus. Its body
was covered with bony plates.
At the end of its tail was a big
lump of bone with spikes, which
Ankylosaurus used as a club.

# Anatosaurus and Corythosaurus

Anatosaurus
(an-*at*-o-*sor*-uss)
about 12 m long

These two dinosaurs are known
as ''duck bills'' because they had
bills or beaks that were broad
and flat, just like a duck's. They
had many rows of teeth for

Corythosaurus
(cor-ith-o-*sor*-uss)
about 9 m long

grinding tough plants.

Corythosaurus had a bony crest on its head that looked like a helmet. Its name means "helmet reptile".

# Protoceratops
(pro-toe-*sair*-a-tops)
nearly 2 m long

Protoceratops had a tough bony collar to protect its neck.

Fossil eggs have been found in Mongolia with the bones of baby Protoceratops inside. Each egg was about 20 cm long.

# Styracosaurus

Styracosaurus
(sty-rak-o-*sor*-uss)
about 4.5 m long

Styracosaurus looked fierce but
it ate plants, not other animals.
It had a beak like a parrot's and
long spikes on its head.

# Tyrannosaurus

Tyrannosaurus
(ty-ran-no-*sor*-uss)
about 12 m long

Tyrannosaurus was the largest
and fiercest meat-eating dinosaur.
Its jaw was over 1 m long and its
teeth were 15 cm long.

# Monoclonius and Triceratops

Monoclonius
(mon-o-*klon*-ee-uss)
about 6 m long

Dinosaurs roamed the Earth for nearly 150 million years. These were two of the last dinosaurs to appear. Triceratops was a plant-eater. It was very big and had two horns above its eyes.

Triceratops
(try-*ser-a*-tops)
about 9 m long

Male Triceratops may have used
these horns to fight, as male
deer do today.

# The first birds

Archaeopteryx
(ar-kee-*op*-terr-iks)
Wing span
about 40 cm

Archaeopteryx was the first bird.
It lived at the time of the
dinosaurs and was about the size
of a magpie.

Archaeopteryx had teeth like a
reptile's. Its long bony tail had
feathers growing on it and its
wings had claws.

# The first mammals

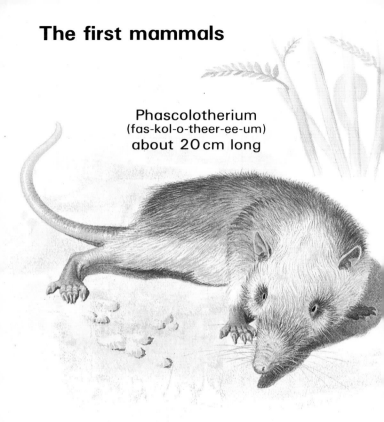

Phascolotherium
(fas-kol-o-theer-ee-um)
about 20 cm long

A mammal is an animal that is
covered with fur and feeds on its
mother's milk when it is young.
The first mammals lived at the
time of the dinosaurs and the
first birds.

Megatherium
(mega-theer-ee-um)
about 5.5 m high

Early mammals, like
Phascolotherium, were no larger
than mice or rats. Later, some
mammals became much bigger.
Megatherium was about 5.5 m
high. It lived in South America.

45

# More mammals

Uintatherium
(oo-in-ta-theer-ee-um)
about 3.5 m long

Uintatherium was as big as an elephant. It looked fierce, but it ate only plants.

**Baluchitherium**
(bal-oo-ki-theer-ee-um)
about 8 m high

Baluchitherium was the tallest
land mammal that has ever lived.
It was about 8 m tall — more than
three times as high as a man,
and it ate leaves and twigs.

47

# Eohippus

(ee-o-hip-puss)

about 30 cm high

Eohippus was the earliest
ancestor of today's horses and
zebras. It was only 30 cm high
and lived in the forests. Although
it had toes instead of hooves, it
could still run very fast.

# Coelodonta
(see-lo-don-ta)

about 2.5 m long

In the Ice Ages, thousands of years ago, much of the Earth was covered in snow and ice. Many types of mammals died of the cold. But Coelodonta, the woolly rhinoceros, had a long, hairy coat to keep it warm.

# Woolly mammoth

about 3 m high
at shoulder

The woolly mammoth was like a huge elephant with a hairy coat. It lived during the Ice Ages. The first humans hunted mammoths for food.

# Sabre-toothed tiger

about 3 m long

This tiger had front teeth about
30 cm long. It could kill a
mammoth or any other animal.
But the first people hunted the
sabre-toothed tiger until there
were none left.

# Index